Dirty Laundry:

Acknowledgements

I am grateful to everybody who has touched my soul in the process of developing my life into what it is at the current moment.

#who are, the doctor, dr. mori jamshidian, Dr. yahya abdul-rahman, katherine isabel vega,
#rocio barajas, ben hashemi, Shahryar Hashemi, Glen Mowlavi, Jocylin Bloodworth, Richard Bloodworth,
#Kevin Kim, Dr. Kevin Nichols, Katherine isabel vega,
#D.R. Artsushi Publishing, Inc., POTUS barack obama, Paulo Coelho, Khalil Ghibran
#eddie bloodworth, kathy bloodworth, VPotus joe biden, carmen cesillia esposito, Mr. carmen esposito
#apartment manager joe,aparment manager patty, veranda apartment fam, mohsin mandavia, rashida mandvi, aisha nawaz
#wajeeha shakeel, carmen navaro, hector navarro jr., hector navarro senior, dianita medina,
#vicente contreras, edgar medina, tia magda jaudegi, "Mrs." Dr. Abdul-Rahman,
#sandra contreras, behzad "uncle bert" hashemi, kamyar "kamy" hashemi, aunt yausi, nestor malagon
#brandon molina, clarissa molina,maryann molina, Arshan Hashemi, Khoa "Casey" Cao
#nelson molina, sig aka sigfredo vega, silvia molina, dr. kevin nichols, francisco vega,
#lidia maria "abuela" vega
#maryon memon, waiz badhar, Dr. Sam Behsetta, "The Dean" Dr.Stephen Goode, The upstairs neighbors.
#rudy (from class), mirna rodriguez, judith (velazquez?), eric "eddie", Taha Monferri?,
#Professor Tyler McMillen, pasha (aunt yassi's nephew), shajin hashemi, sydnew newman
#M.S. Statistics @ Cal State Fullerton, California, Department of Economics @ UC Berkeley
#College of Letter and Science at UC Berekeley, Anaheim, Orange County, Huntington Beach, IFLS
#Vsauce, Michael from Vsauce
#Fullerton
#College of Natural Science and Mathematics at Cal State Fullerton
#amazon, createspace
and many many more.....

Contents:

m

There for a Moment

Welcome, you've arrived!
This is paradise!

It's finally happened because you rolled the dice This
can happen more than twice.

Four-score and twenty year ago I
believed in a clown.

Welcome to uptown Sit
your ass down.

I love it.

A Yellow Key is a Mystery

We were born at the same time When
the universe was created.

Andrea's song is the one that sleeps
Her eyebrows are drawn on high

Eyes eat me in the mirror
Before I hit the shower
I hear a garbage truck outside I
slam the toilet seat open
And pee standing up.
I like it when things are written.
I like basmati rice.
If I liked food that was spit in
Then would never bite.
No one ever dies
Pierced with Life

Inside the mind
A war is fought

No good or evil
Or
Light and dark

Resistance to life's needle

Tearing in
Parting flesh around its point

And in a second the connection is made
And all is complete

Purgatory has deemed
One worthy of redemption.

A Fun Roller-Coaster Ride

In an instant everything was right
And there was nothing left

For the moment we'd survived
To be smothered next

And it was the sweet pleasure of being squeezed.
Of nearly vaporizing in a vacuum.
Having nearly every cell cling to its own identity   with the
grip of a chronic masturbator

that assured we'd move on   we'd keep
going   we'd keep on   up and up.

June Bloom

I have Popped!

I landed in a poor-mouth
And what a dire situation

I had lived up to every situation confronted with

But in the monstrous month of June

I must have been consumed I
must have been in bloom.

Un-Temporary

Certain key connections have been   Seared into
permanence.

The only thing necessary
                              Resides within

To not give up hope
                              Is sufficient
Hear

No more

No less

                              Together risk assumed
To gather failure   doomed

In a wreckage
    Of beauty and grace
                                          I trust in you more
                              than you believe I should

Fail-Safe

Failsafe is secure
                    Failing safely is more

And when we crunched through Halloween

It was clear to see

The distant future touched the recent past.

Welcoming Committee

Locked away and purified
Lead, copper and   Maybe aluminum?

I've read each metal has a journey to complete.
Running away
I sit waiting

Was it a job well done?

Alone I sit   With everyone
Waiting on me

It is a party in my living room.
Because I am not here
Alone

I am everywhere
With you.

Equilibrium

There is nothing left to do.

And yet many tasks have been jotted down

Something unexpected occurred

It was beyond my control

Can I be grateful for the *footloose?*

Locked away and pommeled

        Safely

        In the wild

Where birds sing melodies that rattle my skull.

Like a gong.

It is enriching and strong

        Stockholm Syndrome with the world.

    There is no fight.   Only

equilibrium.

Better Late than Never

Conflict inside the mind.

That must be the source of its existence...I think.

Fighting for what the universe has given is vain.

Live for the wrong reasons.

To dare to care

A small Honda with flare.

A balcony hangs above a parking structure beside

cigarette butts

an affection for those we cannot see in our own moments

of need

brought by the sea is an empty pirate ship

a canoe to rot and feed fish.

This was a dish served cold.

Monkey Me

Monkey see
Monkey do

Monkey pee
Monkey poo

lovely stains our
growing pains

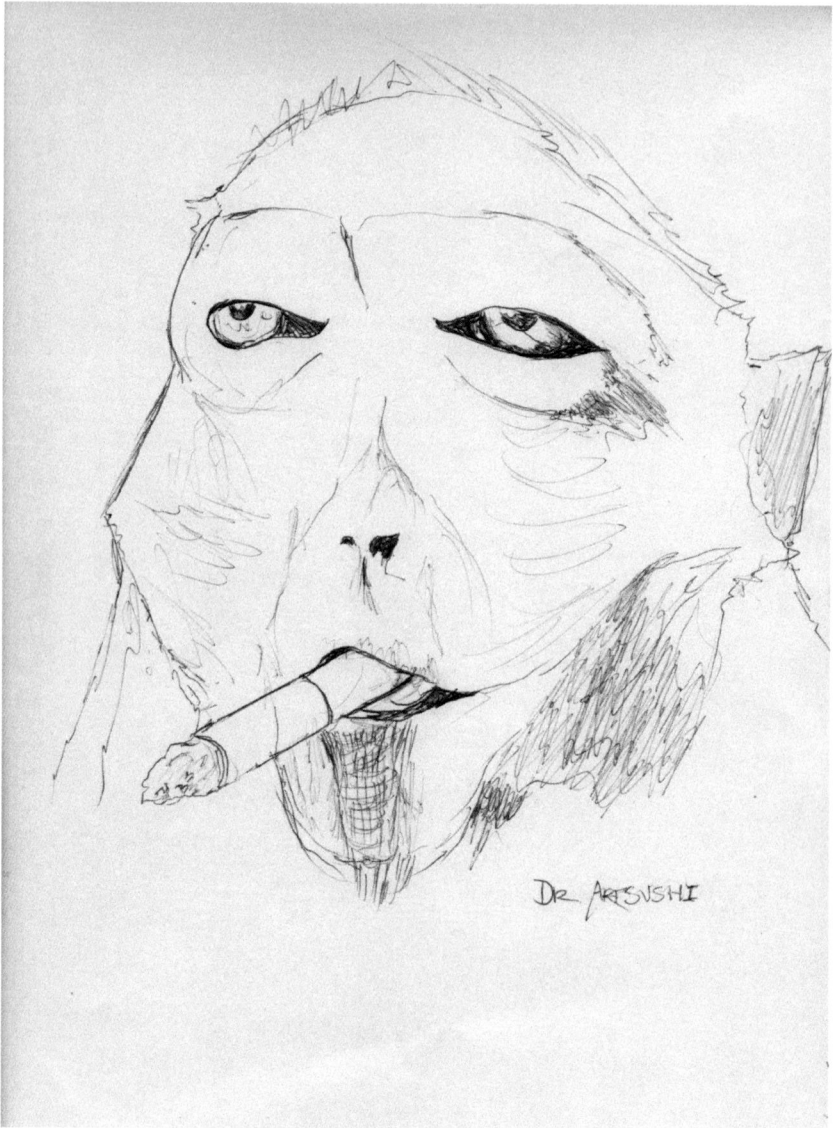

DR ARTSVSHI

Ouch

I hope you like it

Imprecise at times   The mechanism of random energy.

It haunts the paradise of our sleep.

One thousand cigarettes smoked

For a page and a lighter

So that empty cans of soda

Reach their destination

At the dumpsters

Outside my apartment complex

Where

The world is

The bottom half of

The hour glass

And someone else's castle is built.

Godzilla for a Moment

As a kid I was fat

    My cousin was skin and bones.

He said, "You're fat!"

I said,

    "I can survive longer if I'm ever lost without food."

On another occasion we poked sticks into a fire ant hill.

I was bit,

    But pretended like nothing happened.

That eventually got old.

    So we decided to roam his lawn, stomping on mushrooms growing there.

We emulated two Italian brothers we looked up to.

Looking back I realize

We were *Godzilla* for a moment.

Metrics

I espied the future.
Thankful

For hills to climb
And
Troughs to rest in.

It's a blessing.

Crush

I accompanied my mother   to
the department store.

She was thankful I accompanied her
I was wretchedly bored
She handed me her phone.

I played a puzzle game   On the
easiest level.

I crushed it.
Next round

I crushed it

Third round.
I crushed it again.

There was an unbreakable force field.

6 feet in diameter all around me.

Not even a store employee was left standing.

I was an unapproachable god in the ladies shoe section.

Finally a nice older woman asked,
        "Is anybody working here?"

Embarrassed, I grabbed my things and walked away.

Liberation

When things are in balance

The scales will tip   It's okay.

The scales might flip

And

Gravity will cease to exist

Weightless

For the moment

A Super-Positional State of Matter

Blending
With the page
The pen never touches

Ink never completely fills the cartridge inside

There is a void between every atom
That compose the molecules
That compose the organelles
That compose the cells of in my hand

So I write with a pen
Never touching

And in a transcendental state
Waves of light reflect
Off paper

Transforming into particles to be captures by eyes.

A thought is thought

Until it becomes heavy
Until all of matter has rearranged itself

Into a new existence

Motley

It is a big hunch
A motley combination

A penguin
A Seal
A lion
  And wolf

It must be hardwood

Under my feet

Which I can't forget to thank

Pedestrian must always have the right of way.

World Wide Celebration

A celebration within

Without care

It doesn't exist.

That is where I have arrived.

Believing.

Without suffering

There is bliss inside

My illusions become strong

That responsibilities have ceased to exist.

And then I am reminded to suffer.

To hope

And be human again.

So I want to be conscious.

Is it okay?

To make mistakes.

For the moment

I've chosen to hold my celebration.

To hold on and wait a moment
    And

Warm my heart.

I can tuck my chin to my chest

    Waiting to celebrate with the ones I love.

And at every corner I turn

When an unexpected someone's path

    Touches mine.

Even if not a word is spoken.

    I'll warm my heart

Forget my troubles and aknowlegde

    So that when that moment comes to oblige   the

ones you love – you and I   will celebrate

    TOGETHER!!!!

Judging a Book by the Lack of Its Cover

A mask is a mask

But faces melt

At attempts to be saved

So

I guess that's the way I like it.

Watch me at one hundred years old

With a

Thirty two year old's skin.

A Steady Ride

It's a steady ride when we're burning slow.

Extinguishing

The gift god gave us   The skill,

ability and want

to drive.

Gently smothering   our

sun's core

with love.

I'm Taking Sides

Bacon

I don't really understand   The saltiness of
it all.

I prefer sausage
With my breakfast

Bacon is a thin curly piece of burn,
crispy, crunchy savory soot

The nerve of the assumed   masculinity when
ordering   or expressing one's love of bacon
really gets to me.

In my humble opinion
Bacon is hardly a meat

Sausage on the other hand contains   like fifty
thousand animals   all ground up beyond   biological
recognition.

A sausage starts as mystery meat paste   squeezed like
toothpaste
Into a casing that looks like a condom.

So that you can fry them
into crunchy perfection

and once bitten into
that crunchy protection bursts
unleashing meaty goodness into your mouth.

It takes a real pussy-loving American to muster up the courage   look your waitress in
the eyes

and respond
"Sausage please, thank you."

Windowless, Doorless, Seamless

I don't want money
I don't want love

I'd need a drug

I've hardwired   something strong
                          to get me through tonight

a hug

from a beautiful stranger
or an old friend
so my night can feel complete.

Dawn is waiting with a warm embrace,   but night pulls at my
feet.

Still I can't see who I'm asking   To just let me drop
where I stand.
To release me of want   To release me of
need

So I can sleep in peace
Inside a windowless, doorless
white room.

Not for the taking

Your life is not mine to take
And mine is not yours to break

Instantly flashes of passed delights
ancient frights
unforgettable woes

stroke the ego
and tingle the toes

Your life is not mine to take
mine is not yours to make

force feed me the fear
that you've ceased to care

but the crease is fair   in our
feat to share   we are leasing heirs
of the gifts the world   leaves for us

a double edged sword

Your life is not mine

I break.

From right to left

It needs to be violent
Yet harmless

Dynamic
But still

Calculus is movement dissected
Into frozen bits.

us all!   Hallelujah   To

29

Product

The product of imagination
It is real!
The feel of intoxication Can
we want to let it go?
The flow of emancipation
Imagine

The
Mis
guid
ed
Desi
re
to
Win

Thank you I should have felt after I hit the

90 mph ball

At the batting cages.

Instead I raised my head with pride

And lowered it once I got home.

Alone

Feeling sorry for myself

I submitted to the soul of an inatimate object

And teared in shame. Not even

The ball, whose purpose

In this world

Is to be thrown

Struck

And slowly die

For us to live

sided with me that night.

Shit Out of Luck

(Barnacle Weaver)

One day I broke into a sprint.

I was on a bullet train
A one way trip

I didn't check to see if my shoe laces were untied.
I just hauled ass.

I ran to a job interview
And crashed through the glass door

And then ran back home to give my mom a high five.

At least I think it was my mom.
I couldn't tell to be honest. It was a blur.

Oh well, I saw an open hand in front of me and slapped the shit out of it.

I ran to friend's house that day.

He had just gotten off work.

Understandably he was tired and didn't feel like doing much.
So I ran circles around him until he kicked me out.

I thought, "To hell with sleep."

So I kept running.

I was an invincible, indominable, abomination

Then one day my shoe felt loose and I was forced to sit down a while.

My shoe laces had snapped right as I was approaching warp speed.

I needed to get some new shoe laces, or new shoes, or at least change my shoes.
But I had no time for that.

And I probably did, but I had been running for so long I couldn't remember where I'd placed the *rest* of my stuff.

So I threw half of the broken shoelace away. Carefully laced my shoe with the remaining half,
Going through half the holes in a diagonal fashion.
There was enough of the shoelace left

To bring one end of the lace from the top right corner and the other from the bottom left corner
To tie in the center.

BAM!!

I was back on my way.
I ran and ran.
Then suddenly, I couldn't run anymore.

So I walked back home.
There I loved.
There I stayed.

Punctuality

I want to lay on the floor
Next to you
With the door open
Until the sun sets
Love's fatality

Asymmetry

If Sacred texts
                open doors to alternate realities
                or make possible impossibilities

        Then why do insects   plague the floors with
bankruptcy and duality.

        God cut his wrist   to discover how much the
wound would bleed.

        And so I believe that's where we get

        Curiosity
Need   and
        Shame

        To fill our being until we are all together again.

Prophetear

To protect as a protégé
only that is proper.

Prone to disappear.
Prominent in the clear.

The legend of a profiteer.

Grunge Works

I got to make it work.

I got to make it go

I got to make it fit

I got to make it

And I don't even care, who's there

to see it.

Will it be some of you   who aimed to

be my friends

or

will it be my turn

to burn amongst the tyrants   the ones

who seemed to dare.   The ones who seemed to

know   exactly what was theirs.

I was dreaming.

Taz

A subtle rage fills me in.
And lets me know what is what
on the street.

And as a fury grows,
I fear it becomes obsolete.

Nothing so extreme is needed   in burger
land home of the free.

Expression is costly   when
succession is cheap.

And lastly and least
I stand on my feet

Forcing me in
admitting defeat.

Rhythm's Shadow's Vibration

We are but a mere blink in the universe's perspective.

No, we are less than that.

We are but a fraction of a thoughtless thought.   A
thought which is forgotten before even realized in the mind   of the
world's architect.

We are not here nor there

Not now or then

"See you later!" will come to pass

"I saw you there" will be forgotten.

In time's life line our birth is non-existent

Our death therefore an impossibility!

Savor this moment.

Now forget it.

Live and don't think about it.

Love but don't prefer

Prefer, but please be equal

Equate; there's no answer

Learn, but don't memorize.

Remember but don't reminisce.

Live and don't think about it.

After all, we're nothing

But a

Rhythm's Shadow's Vibration.

Internal Ore

I am yours for the taking.
After being discarded

The purpose for which I was originally built
has become obsolete.

Take me into your furnace.
Its grill is porous ceramic and it is used to grind me down
It projects your inner glow.
Then spit me out.

If you've raked and weeded where I once stood.
You'll see my core seeded good   with your intentions,
ambitions, and mud.

out fits too, but not for you.

This must be what trash feels   when
it is being reborn.   Crushed broken and
melted down   into liquid form.

becoming a fine glass for you to drink from.

Restless Summer's Day

A restless summer day   belongs
to the dude that drowned.
It shook the Earth
when Atlas frowned.

And all the pain there existed was absorbed
by shades of brown.

It reminds me of the stone in mecca.
It once was white.
It has been touched by sinners' hands
Into blackened fright.

Carried

I remember my grandma

She would cut her juice with water.

She said it was too sweet otherwise.

That's how much she loved me.   She told me

that when I stretched

I grew taller.

She told me the moon fell in love with the sun

Although they were on opposite ends of the earth.

She called me brave.

Whenever I asked her for a story, she obliged.

And I was always the protagonist

She's been gone for a while now.

But I'll never forget

The love I grew

Accustomed to.

Dirty Laundry

Kathy sorted the laundry.

She expressed her discomfort, "It smells really bad!"

It was then I realized a billion galaxies had come to fruition

Been extinguished

And still billions more were being born.

From a fraction of a fraction of a DNA strand

of a bacteria   on a

thread   from my underwear

that was born on

my gooch

Sure Lock Homes

These moments where everybody
Obviously knows something I don't.

Is when I realize, that
the world is sorting itself out
after my miscalculated steps.

But then it also is fixing itself
After you walked in the door.

So remember
You were fat at the start of November.

Don't blame me for gaining weight
During the holidays.

Cost of Translation

I want to translate the universe.
While I float through infinity.

But all I can express is an alien arm.
Bony, scaly and tired
Offering a bouquet of flowers.

Held together at the pettals
by a stringy spider web.

So I guess, I am thankful.

We Gave Up Paradise for Knowledge

In a Serpeant We Trusted

I am fucking ignorant   but it's

okay

with reason to write   no

purposeful rhyme

by chance I make a point   while

making no sence.

Joint rhymes with point   but

I'm smoking a cigarette

I have to quit.

Just another thought

Make another phrase

no reasoning rhyme   it's

seasoning time

I should be asleep, but I am awake.

My skull is for brains kept

My brain is for thoughts stored

Self aware

Human form

Mistakes no erased
Human form

Acid Washed

A panoramic view of the city lies ahead.

A million city lights blaring up, there was no need to see the sky

And then I looked down to see the earth below me.

Always I'd wanted an Ant Farm

I realized I had one.

no queen, no common good, no mutual goal

millions of busy ants working   busy, strong and

beautifully pitiful

harmoniously accomplishing individually

The most important things are short and sweet

The most important things are simple

Simply understood but not simply there for the taking.

A panoramic view from the earth.

I look up to see the sky.

When I was a child I thought it simple to go to space.

I thought I'd go some day. Maybe I still will.

I never thought of the precision, patience, and strength needed for such a feat.

I always wanted to be in space.

I realized I'm floating in it

And I am full of it.

The most valued things are complex.

Complex by design, difficult to understand, and intricately constructed.

The most powerful things are concrete

Hard to obtain, tough to explain, laboriously recognized in all obscurity

A simple piece of paper, intricately designed, destroys the world one soul at a time

I walk back down and take my place.

Don't Forget

Build a Tomb

The man on the moon made his own tomb.

His dreams and his wishes

He packed his guitar.

He gathered his luggage and jumped in his car.

The man on the moon shot for the stars.

He left all behind; He shot for the stars.

Rockets and whistles into the sky

He shot for the stars, only to reach the moon.

Or did he aim for the moon miss and drift into space?

I don't remember, but this is the case

of the man on the moon

and the dream that he chased.

When I Step Back

Forgive my haste.

My life is meant to love you.

I have my life's entirety to do so.

Forgive my taste.

I am abrasive and displaced

I served you better by not serving at all.

I don't know what a soul is, but I'm sure ours have touched.

Tangled in a knot.

I am confused love.

Tell me I'm right.

Tell me my love is unjustifiable, undeniable and irresistible

And tell me it's okay.

An Unstoppable Current

An unstoppable current of thoughts form waves of suffocating Ideas.
And as I tumble in the ocean of my mind, like dry clothes frying in a dryer
Titanic waves force me to surrender.

I hold my breath hoping to surface alive.
My face feels fresh with the wind flowing across it.

That is my signal to breath a breathe of relief.
I gasp for air

Only to be swallowed again.

Understood

In all honesty, I never understood.
You are kind, you are wise; You are true friend.

Though now we are worlds apart, your friendship is enough to conquer both.
You must have ears like an elephant under that elegant scarf.

You've heard me whine and you've listened.
Thank you for that.

Your patience has kept me sane.
In my vanity you've sat
Self-pity and all.
I guess that makes sense because
I am Sexy, Persian and Tall.

To me you are gold.
Like being nine years old, and eating your favorite breakfast cereal
Out of your favorite cereal bowl.

Plus I'd totally do you now fuck off.

From The Ashes Rose the Phoenix

My heart lays in a drawer next to my bed.

In a million pieces, it is carefully collected like sweepings in a dust pan

It used to be big and strong and proudly displayed to the world.

Now it blends in with the dirt that so many have done to it.

It serves no purpose and only a few will ever see it.

So, keep in mind if you venture into my bedroom in search of my heart   chances are the only thing you'll find is my mind.

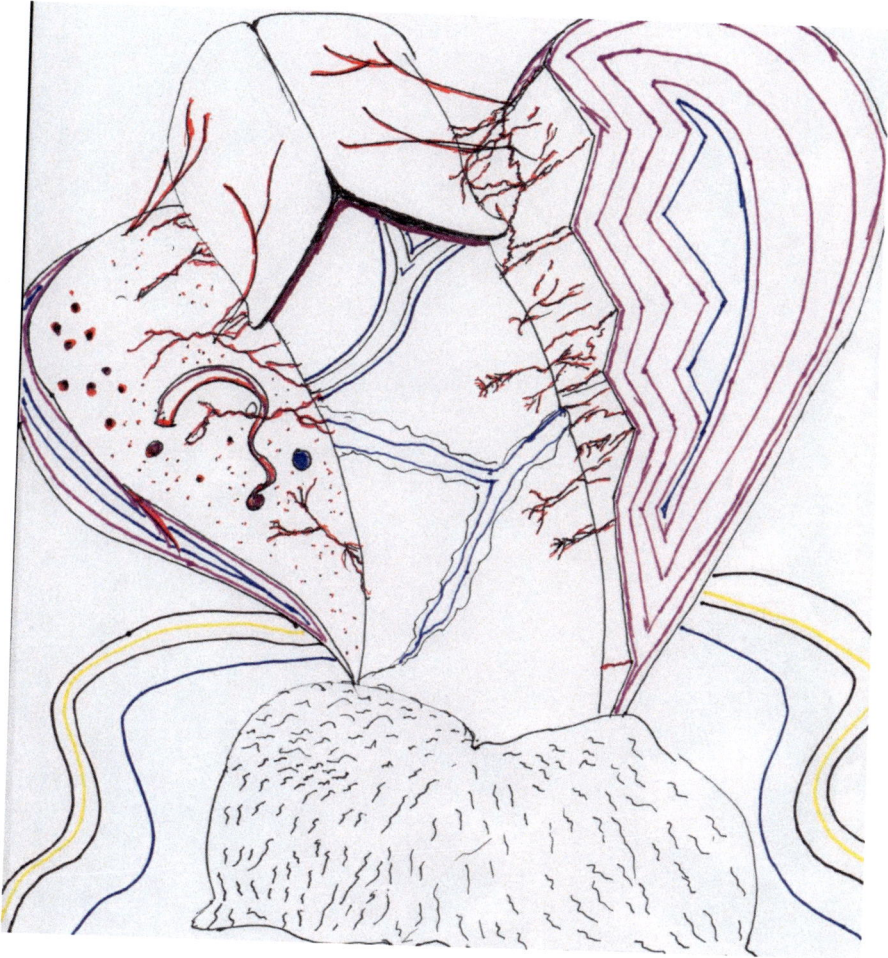

Made in the USA
Las Vegas, NV
25 June 2022